Way Cool Drinks

by Marilyn LaPenta

Consultant:
Sharon Richter, MS, RD, CDN

BEARPORT
PUBLISHING

NEW YORK, NEW YORK

Credits

All food illustrations by Kim Jones. Photo, p.13: © Tomaspavelka/Dreamstime.com.

Publisher: Kenn Goin
Senior Editor: Lisa Wiseman
Creative Director: Spencer Brinker
Design: Debrah Kaiser

Library of Congress Cataloging-in-Publication Data

LaPenta, Marilyn.
  Way cool drinks / by Marilyn LaPenta ; consultant, Sharon Richter.
    p. cm. — (Yummy tummy recipes)
  Includes bibliographical references and index.
  ISBN-13: 978-1-61772-163-2 (lib. bdg.)
  ISBN-10: 1-61772-163-8 (lib. bdg.)
  1. Fruit drinks. 2. Cookbooks. I. Title.
  TX815.F78L32 2012
  641.8'75—dc23

                    2011017444

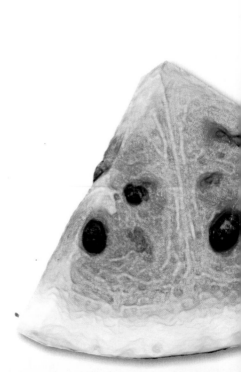

For more information, write to Bearport Publishing Company, Inc., 45 West 21st Street, Suite 3B, New York, New York 10010. Printed in the United States of America in North Mankato, Minnesota.

070111
042711CGB

10 9 8 7 6 5 4 3 2 1

Contents

Making Healthy Cool Drinks

Get ready to prepare some yummy recipes for your tummy! The colorful beverage concoctions in *Way Cool Drinks* are super easy to make. If you serve them in drinking glasses that have fun shapes and use silly straws, paper umbrellas, and other decorations—you're ready for a party!

The great thing about making your own food is that you know exactly what goes into it. Many **pre-made** foods that you buy in grocery stores have ingredients to **preserve** them. These preservatives are not always good for your body. Often pre-made foods are also made with more sugar and fat than needed. Many people already have too much fat and sugar in their diets—which may lead to **obesity**. Use the ideas on page 22 for making the nutritious and tasty drinks in this book even healthier.

Getting Started

Use these cooking tips and safety and tool guidelines to make the best drinks you've ever tasted.

Tips

Here are a few tips to get your cooking off to a great start.

- Quickly check out the Prep Time, Tools, and Servings information at the top of each recipe. It will tell you how long the recipe takes to prepare, the tools you'll need, and the number of people the recipe serves.

- Once you pick a recipe, set out the tools and ingredients that you will need on your worktable.

- Before and after cooking, wash your hands well with warm soapy water to kill any germs.

- Wash fruit, as appropriate, to get rid of any dirt or chemicals.

- Put on an apron or smock to protect your clothes.

- Roll up long shirtsleeves to keep them clean.

- Tie back long hair or cover it to keep it out of the food.

- *Very Important:* Keep the adults happy and clean up the kitchen when you've finished cooking.

PREP TIME · **TOOLS** · **SERVINGS** · **INGREDIENTS** · **RECIPE**

10 Minutes Prep Time · Tools · **2** Servings

Ingredients

1 cup mango, cut into 1-inch cubes
1 cup pineapple, cut into 1-inch cubes
½ cup **sliced** strawberries

8 ice cubes
2 whole strawberries

Steps

1. If you are not using a pre-cut mango, ask an adult to use the knife to slice the mango in half on the cutting board. Then remove the pit. Have him or her cut lines into each side of the fruit in a checkerboard pattern, without cutting through the skin. Gently push on the mango skin, and the cubes inside will pop up—ready to be sliced off. Then have the adult cut the pineapple into cubes.

2. Put the mango and pineapple cubes in the blender. Blend on high for 1 minute.

3. If you are not using pre-sliced strawberries, pull the stems and leaves off the fruit. Ask an adult to slice them in half on the cutting board.

4. Add the sliced strawberries to the blender and blend on high for 10 seconds.

5. Add the ice cubes and CRUSH in the blender for 30 seconds.

6. Pour the mixture into the 2 glasses.

7. Take the 2 whole strawberries and ask an adult to make a slit in each one. Then slip one onto the rim of each glass.

Most mangoes are grown in tropical countries such as Brazil. However, U.S. farmers in Florida, California, and Hawaii grow some mangoes, too.

Be Safe

Keep these safety tips in mind while you are in the kitchen.

- If the food must be cut up with a knife or peeled with a peeler, ask an adult for help.

- Get an adult's permission to use a blender. Make sure an adult is present when using this appliance.

- Make sure the blender is turned off before adding ingredients.

- Never plug or unplug a blender with wet hands.

- Never stick your hands in a blender.

- Always make sure the lid is on tight before starting the blender. Turn off the blender before removing the lid.

Tools You Need

Here's a guide to the tools you will need to make the various recipes in this book.

Small glass, 8 ounces

Paper cup, 8 ounces

Straw

Medium glass, 12 ounces

Large glass, 16 ounces

Punch bowl and ladle

Measuring cup

Measuring spoons

Spoon

Ice cream scoop

Cutting board

Knife

Apple or vegetable peeler

Blender

Long toothpick

Small plate

Ring mold or ice cube tray

Blue Melon Medley

10 Minutes Prep Time

Tools

2 Servings

Ingredients

2 cups seedless watermelon, cut into 1-inch cubes

1 cup cantaloupe, cut into 1-inch cubes

¼ cup pineapple juice

1 cup blueberries

8 ice cubes

Steps

1. If you are not using pre-cut watermelon, then have an adult use a knife to cut the watermelon into 1-inch cubes on the cutting board. Do the same for the cantaloupe.

2. Pour the pineapple juice into the blender. Put aside two watermelon cubes and add the rest to the blender. **Blend** on high for 30 seconds.

3. Put the blueberries and cantaloupe in the blender. Blend on high for 1 minute or until the mixture is smooth.

4. Add the ice cubes to the mixture in the blender and CRUSH for 30 seconds.

5. Pour the mixture into the glasses.

6. Take the 2 extra watermelon cubes and place them on the rim of each glass for decoration. Then pop in a straw and you're ready to slurp!

Health Tip

Research has shown that blueberries have more **antioxidants** than most other fruits. Some scientists and doctors believe that antioxidants may slow or possibly prevent the development of diseases such as cancer.

Originally from Africa and India, cantaloupe was first brought to North America by Christopher Columbus, an explorer from Italy, in 1494.

Red Lava Volcano

2 Minutes Prep Time

Tools

1 Serving

Ingredients

1 cup cran-raspberry juice

1 cup seltzer

1 scoop raspberry sherbet

Steps

1. Place the glass on top of the plate.

2. Pour the cran-raspberry juice into the glass.

3. Add the seltzer.

4. Scoop the raspberry sherbet into the glass and stir with the spoon.

5. Watch the seltzer bubble up and flow over the glass just like lava erupting from a volcano.

6. Add a straw to help you drink this messy treat.

Lava is the liquid rock that flows out of a volcano when it erupts. It can be as hot as 2,200° F.

Health Tip

Sherbets contain milk or cream, which adds fat to the recipe. To reduce the fat in your volcano, try **sorbet**. It is usually fat-free.

Favorite Fruit Punch

5 Minutes Prep Time

Tools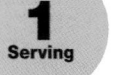

1 Serving

Ingredients

4 ice cubes

¼ cup seltzer

A dash of concentrated lemon juice

¼ cup cranberry juice cocktail

¼ cup pineapple juice

¼ cup orange juice

Steps

1. Put the ice cubes in the glass and then pour in the seltzer, the concentrated lemon juice, and the cranberry juice cocktail.

2. Pour the pineapple juice into one measuring cup and the orange juice into the other measuring cup.

3. Take a measuring cup in each hand and pour the orange juice and pineapple juice into the glass at the same time.

4. Mix with the spoon and enjoy this refreshing drink.

Health Tip

Some studies have shown that cranberries may help prevent **plaque** from forming on your teeth.

Cranberries are also known as "bounceberries," because when a fresh cranberry is dropped, it bounces.

Mango Tango

Health Tip

Use frozen fruit if you don't have fresh. As long as it doesn't have added sugar, frozen fruit is just as healthy for you.

10 Minutes Prep Time

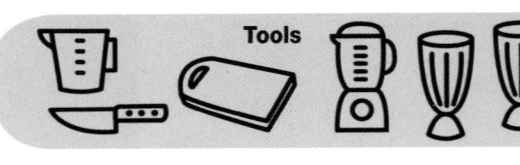
Tools

2 Servings

Ingredients

1 cup mango, cut into 1-inch cubes

1 cup pineapple, cut into 1-inch cubes

½ cup **sliced** strawberries

8 ice cubes

2 whole strawberries

Steps

1. If you are not using a pre-cut mango, ask an adult to use the knife to slice the mango in half on the cutting board. Then remove the pit. Have him or her cut lines into each side of the fruit in a checkerboard pattern, without cutting through the skin. Gently push on the mango skin, and the cubes inside will pop up—ready to be sliced off. Then have the adult cut the pineapple into cubes.

2. Put the mango and pineapple cubes in the blender. Blend on high for 1 minute.

3. If you are not using pre-sliced strawberries, pull the stems and leaves off the fruit. Ask an adult to slice them in half on the cutting board.

4. Add the sliced strawberries to the blender and blend on high for 10 seconds.

5. Add the ice cubes and CRUSH in the blender for 30 seconds.

6. Pour the mixture into the 2 glasses.

7. Take the 2 whole strawberries and ask an adult to make a slit in each one. Then slip one onto the rim of each glass.

Most mangoes are grown in tropical countries such as Brazil. However, U.S. farmers in Florida, California, and Hawaii grow some mangoes, too.

11

Fruit Fusion

5 Minutes Prep Time

Tools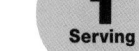

1 Serving

Ingredients

¼ cup grape juice

¼ cup pineapple juice

½ cup cran-raspberry juice

1 tablespoon frozen apple juice concentrate

6 ice cubes

Steps

1. Pour the grape juice, pineapple juice, cran-raspberry juice, and frozen apple juice concentrate into the blender. Blend on high for 10 seconds.

2. Add the ice cubes and CRUSH in the blender for 30 seconds.

3. Pour into the glass and add a fun straw.

This foamy drink changes colors. It starts off light pink. After two minutes, the bottom part of the drink turns red—right before your eyes!

Health Tip

Though they may be small, grapes are an excellent source of **manganese**, which the body needs to stay healthy.

100% organic

APPLE JUICE

Kiwi Concoction

5 Minutes Prep Time

Tools

1 Serving

Ingredients

1 kiwi, peeled and sliced

1 frozen banana, cut into pieces*

⅓ cup orange juice

⅓ cup lemonade

⅓ cup seltzer

(*Note: To freeze a banana, peel it and then break it into pieces. Seal the pieces inside a freezer-safe container or plastic bag and store in the freezer for at least a few hours.)

Steps

1. Ask an adult to use the knife to cut off the ends of the kiwi on the cutting board. Throw the ends away. Then ask him or her to cut one slice of the kiwi with the skin still on it. Put the slice off to the side.

2. Peel the rest of the kiwi and then have an adult slice it.

3. Put the kiwi and the frozen banana pieces in the blender. Also add the orange juice and lemonade. Blend on high for 30 seconds or until smooth.

4. Add the seltzer. Blend for 5 seconds more.

5. Pour the drink into the glass and attach the slice of kiwi with the skin still on it to the rim of the glass.

a kiwi bird ▶

Kiwis are named after the kiwi bird, the national bird of New Zealand. The fruit got its name because its brown fuzzy skin looks similar to the bird's brown feathers.

Health Tip

For a healthier drink, keep the skin on the kiwi. It's **edible** and full of **fiber**, which can help you maintain a healthy heart.

13

Winter Wonder Punch

10 Minutes Prep Time*

Tools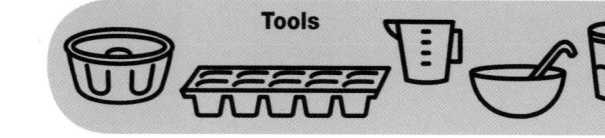

10-12 Servings

* The frozen ring mold must be prepared the night before.

Ingredients

12-ounce package frozen strawberries

Water (enough to fill the ring mold almost to the top, leaving a ½ inch space)

12-ounce can frozen lemonade, **undiluted**

12-ounce can frozen limeade, undiluted

2 quarts ginger ale

2 cups lime sherbet (or sorbet)

Steps

1. The night before you plan on making the punch, spread out the frozen strawberries in the ring mold. Fill the mold with water, leaving a ½ inch space at the top. Then put the ring mold into the freezer and leave it overnight. If you don't have a ring mold, put the strawberries into an ice cube tray, fill with water, and freeze overnight. You may need to have an adult slice the strawberries so they fit in the tray.

2. The next day, mix the frozen lemonade, limeade, and the ginger ale in the punch bowl.

3. When you are ready to drink the punch, add the lime sherbet. Watch the punch fizz.

4. Now it's time to add the ring of strawberries. To do so, take the ring mold out of the freezer and carefully dip the bottom of it into warm water for 10 seconds. Then turn it upside down and gently shake the mold so that the frozen strawberry ring pops out. Place the ring in the punch bowl, allowing it to float on top of the punch. If you used an ice cube tray, pop the cubes out of the tray and place in the punch bowl.

5. Use the **ladle** to scoop the punch into the cups.

Health Tip

Strawberries are an excellent source of antioxidants that are heart healthy.

There are more than 600 varieties of strawberries. They can differ in size, flavor, and texture.

Summer Slushy

5 Minutes Prep Time

 Tools

1 Serving

Ingredients

1 cup ice cubes

1 cup seedless watermelon, cut into 1-inch cubes

1 teaspoon honey

Steps

1. Put the ice cubes in the blender and CRUSH until the ice becomes slushy.

2. If you are not using pre-cut watermelon, then ask an adult to cut the watermelon with the knife into 1-inch cubes on the cutting board.

3. Add the watermelon and honey to the blender. Blend on high for 5 seconds.

4. Pour the slushy into the glass and eat it with a spoon. You can also put it in a paper cup and squeeze out the tasty treat!

Watermelon **quenches** your thirst because it is about 90 percent water. Ancient explorers didn't carry **canteens**. Instead, they carried watermelon as their source of water.

Health Tip

Try using honey instead of table sugar in the foods you eat. Honey is sweeter so you will use less of it. It also contains important **vitamins**.

Blueberry Bash Smoothie

10 Minutes Prep Time

Tools

2 Servings

Ingredients

6 ounces vanilla yogurt

⅓ cup milk

⅓ cup pineapple juice

⅔ cup blueberries

6 ice cubes

Steps

1. Put the yogurt, milk, and pineapple juice in the blender. Blend on high for 10 seconds.

2. Add the blueberries to the blender, setting 8 to 12 of them off to the side. Blend on high for 10 more seconds.

3. Add the ice and CRUSH for 30 seconds.

4. Pour the mixture into the glasses.

5. To make this drink even cooler, create blueberry **kebabs**. To do this, take 2 long toothpicks and put on each one the blueberries that you set aside. Then place a kebab across the top of each glass.

Native Americans called blueberries "Star Berries," because the five points of a blueberry blossom make a star shape.

Health Tip

Pineapple is an excellent source of **vitamin C** and manganese, which can help keep your bones strong and healthy.

Banana Bonanza

5 Minutes Prep Time

Tools

1 Serving

Ingredients

1 kiwi, peeled and sliced

½ cup sliced strawberries

6 ounces vanilla or strawberry yogurt

1 frozen banana, cut into pieces (See page 13 for prep.)

3 whole strawberries

Steps

1. Peel the kiwi and ask an adult to use the knife to slice it on the cutting board. Put 2 slices of the kiwi off to the side.

2. If you are not using pre-sliced strawberries, pull the leaves and stems off the whole berries. Ask an adult to slice the berries in half.

3. Put the sliced strawberries and kiwi in the blender. Blend on high for 20 seconds or until the mixture is smooth.

4. Add the yogurt. Blend on high for 10 seconds.

5. Add the frozen banana pieces to the mixture and blend until the mixture is smooth.

6. Pour the drink into the glass.

7. To make this drink even more fun, add the whole strawberries and slices of kiwi that you set aside to the toothpick to make a fruit kebab. Then place the kebab across the top of the glass.

A cluster of 10 to 20 bananas is called a hand. Each banana is known as a finger.

Health Tip

Bananas are considered one of the best sources of **potassium**, which is necessary for healthy muscles.

Peachango Paradise

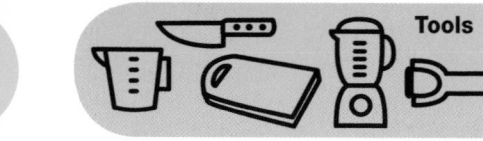

10 Minutes Prep Time

Tools

2 Servings

Ingredients

1 cup mango, cut into pieces

1 peach, peeled and cut into pieces

6 ounces vanilla yogurt

6 ice cubes

Steps

1. If you are not using a pre-cut mango, ask an adult to use the knife to slice the mango in half on the cutting board. Then remove the pit. Have him or her cut lines into each side of the fruit in a checkerboard pattern, without cutting through the skin. Gently push on the mango skin, and the cubes inside will pop up—ready to be sliced off. (See the cut-up mango picture on page 11.)

2. Put the mango pieces in the blender. Blend on high for 20 seconds or until the mixture is smooth.

3. If you are not using a pre-cut peach, first use the peeler to peel it. Then ask an adult to cut the peach into pieces.

4. Add the peach pieces to the blender and blend on high for about 20 seconds or until smooth.

5. Put the vanilla yogurt in the blender and blend on high for 10 seconds.

6. Add the ice cubes to the mixture in the blender and CRUSH for 30 seconds.

7. Pour the mixture into 2 glasses. If you like, add a fun straw.

Peaches come in different shapes. Some are round like a ball and others are so flat that they look like hockey pucks.

Health Tip

Peaches are a good source of **vitamin A** and fiber.

18

Spring Berry Fling

5 Minutes Prep Time

Tools

1 Serving

Ingredients

1 cup of your favorite berries (strawberries, raspberries, blueberries, or blackberries)

¾ cup vanilla yogurt or frozen vanilla yogurt

4 ice cubes

Steps

1. Put almost all the berries, keeping a few off to the side, and all the yogurt or frozen yogurt in the blender and blend on high for 20 seconds.

2. Add the ice cubes and CRUSH for 30 seconds.

3. Pour the mixture into the glass. For decoration, make a berry kebab with the leftover berries using the toothpick.

Health Tip

Don't be fooled by a raspberry's size. This small fruit packs in lots of fiber as well as vitamins, such as vitamin C, in every bite.

Though the most common type of raspberry is reddish in color, these berries also come in black, purple, orange, yellow, and white.

Apple Cinnamon Swirl

15 Minutes Prep Time

Tools

1 Serving

Ingredients

1 Granny Smith apple, peeled and sliced

¼ cup **chopped** walnuts

6 ounces vanilla yogurt

6 ice cubes

A dash of cinnamon

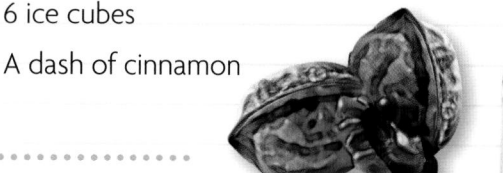

Steps

1. If you are not using a pre-sliced apple, peel the apple. Then ask an adult to slice it with the knife on the cutting board. Throw out the seeds and the **core**.

2. Put the apple slices, walnuts, and yogurt in the blender. Blend on high for 30 seconds.

3. Add the ice cubes and CRUSH in the blender for 30 seconds.

4. Pour the mixture into the glass.

5. Sprinkle the cinnamon on top and swirl it around with the toothpick, making an S shape in the drink.

There are 7,500 kinds of apples grown around the world. About 2,500 types are grown in the United States.

Chocolate Peanut Butter Shake

5 Minutes Prep Time

Tools

1 Serving

Ingredients

¾ cup milk

¾ cup frozen chocolate yogurt

2 tablespoons smooth peanut butter

1 frozen banana, cut into pieces
(See page 13 for prep.)

Steps

1. Pour the milk into the blender. Add the frozen yogurt and the peanut butter. Blend on high for 30 seconds.

2. Add the frozen banana and CRUSH in the blender for 30 seconds or until smooth.

3. Pour the drink into the glass and add a crazy-shaped straw.

Peanuts are not actually nuts—they are **legumes** and they grow underground.

Health Tip

If you are allergic to peanut butter, ask an adult if you can try other nut butters, such as almond, cashew, or sunflower.

Healthy Tips

Always Read Labels

Labels tell how much fat, sugar, and other nutrients are in food. If you compare one bottle of juice with another, you can determine which one has the most **calories**, sugar, vitamins, and so on.

Make Recipe Substitutions

While all the recipes in this book call for wholesome ingredients, you can often reduce the calories in the drinks by substituting ingredients that are lower in fat and sugar. For example:

Fat: use nonfat or **low-fat** yogurt instead of regular yogurt; use low-fat or skim milk instead of whole milk.

Sugar: with an adult's permission, use reduced-calorie juices instead of regular juices; add more ice and cut the amount of juices for a less sweet, more healthful treat; always use 100% fruit juice with no added sugar.

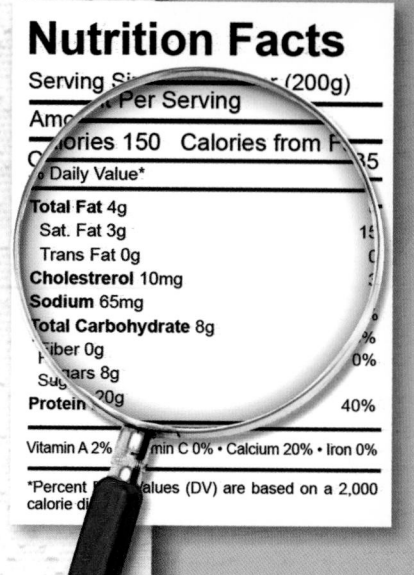

Nutrition Facts

Serving Si___ ___ (200g)

___ ___ Per Serving

Amo___

___ories 150   Calories from F___ __5

% Daily Value*

Total Fat 4g

  Sat. Fat 3g   1__

  Trans Fat 0g   0

Cholestrerol 10mg

Sodium 65mg

Total Carbohydrate 8g

  Fiber 0g   %

  Sugars 8g   0%

Protein 20g   40%

Vitamin A 2% • ___min C 0% • Calcium 20% • Iron 0%

*Percent ___ Values (DV) are based on a 2,000 calorie di___

100% Cranberry Juice NO SUGAR ADDED!

LOW FAT

Glossary

antioxidants (*an*-tee-OK-suh-duhnts) a group of substances found in certain foods that may prevent cell damage in people and animals; damage to cells can cause disease

blend (BLEND) to mix two or more ingredients together

blossom (BLOSS-uhm) a flower on a fruit tree or other plant

calories (KAL-uh-reez) measurements of the amount of energy that food provides

canteens (kan-TEENZ) small portable containers for holding water or other liquids

chopped (CHOPT) cut into little pieces

core (KOR) the hard center of an apple or pear where the seeds are found

edible (ED-uh-buhl) able to be eaten

fiber (FYE-bur) a substance found in parts of plants that when eaten passes through the body but is not completely digested; it helps food move through one's intestines and is important for good health

kebabs (kuh-BOBS) small pieces of food placed on skewers or sticks

ladle (LAY-duhl) a large, deep spoon with a very long handle

legumes (LEG-yoomz) plants with seeds that grow in pods; for example, peanuts and beans

low-fat (*loh*-FAT) food that has three or fewer grams of fat per serving

manganese (MANG-uh-neez) a mineral found in foods such as kale, pineapple, raspberries, and grapes

obesity (oh-BEESS-uh-tee) a condition where a person is extremely overweight

plaque (PLAK) a coating that can form on one's teeth caused by food or bacteria; can cause tooth decay

potassium (puh-TASS-ee-uhm) a mineral that is necessary for the body's growth, especially for one's muscles; found in bananas, potatoes, and other fruits and vegetables

pre-made (PREE-mayd) already prepared

preserve (pri-ZURV) to treat food with something, such as a chemical, so that it doesn't spoil

quenches (KWENCH-iz) satisfies one's thirst

sliced (SLYEST) cut into thin, flat pieces

sorbet (sor-BAY) a frozen dessert made with fruit juice

undiluted (*uhn*-duh-LOOT-id) without added water

vitamin A (VYE-tuh-min AY) a type of vitamin found in sweet potatoes, spinach, peaches, and other foods; helps preserve and improve eyesight

vitamin C (VYE-tuh-min SEE) a type of vitamin found in fruits and vegetables; it's important for healing the body and for keeping teeth and bones strong

vitamins (VYE-tuh-minz) substances in food that are necessary for good health

Index

Bibliography

Chance, Daniella. *More Smoothies for Life: Satisfy, Energize, and Heal Your Body.* New York: Clarkson Potter (2007).

Rutherford, Tracy. *Smoothies: Healthy Shakes & Blends.* Boston: Periplus Editions (2003).

Read More

Rockwell, Lizzy. *Good Enough to Eat: A Kid's Guide to Food and Nutrition.* New York: HarperCollins (2009).

Sears, William and Martha, and Christy Watts Kelly. *Eat Healthy, Feel Great.* New York: Little Brown for Young Readers (2002).

Learn More Online

To learn more about making cool drinks, visit
www.bearportpublishing.com/YummyTummyRecipes

About the Author

Marilyn LaPenta has been a teacher for more than 25 years and has published numerous works for teachers and students. She has always enjoyed cooking with her students and her three children. Marilyn lives in Brightwaters, New York, with her husband, Philip.